THE SEA
WALKS
INTO A
WALL

ANNE
KENNEDY

THE SEA
WALKS
INTO A
WALL

 AUCKLAND
UNIVERSITY
PRESS

First published 2021
Reprinted 2022
Auckland University Press
University of Auckland
Private Bag 92019
Auckland 1142
New Zealand
www.aucklanduniversitypress.co.nz

ISBN 978 1 86940 958 6

Published with the assistance of Creative New Zealand

ARTS COUNCIL OF NEW ZEALAND TOI AOTEAROA

A catalogue record for this book is available from the National Library
of New Zealand

Cover design and artwork by Philip Kelly
Internal design by Carolyn Lewis

This book was printed on FSC® certified paper

Printed in Auckland by Ligare Ltd

For Elizabeth Caffin

whose editorial vision has lit my way

Contents

The house is quiet now
And still.

No gale from the sea
No weeping in the garden
Or cry from the hill.

Later there will be
Stars and a moon
Tomorrow the sun.

J. C. Sturm, 'Untitled'

1

Flood Monologue

You never discussed the stream
and no doubt the stream didn't want

your discourse (its own merry way)
but now that you live by the stream

a mosquito has come up the bank
and bitten you, and the stream

is in your bloodstream. You buff
the site of entry like a trophy

Your chuckling new acquaintance
takes your cells out to the sea.

*

It goes all night, you tell your friends
drinking wine to warm the house

(already warm), and laugh of course
like a drain. Later in your roomy

queen you listen to its monologue –
ascending plane that never reaches

altitude. Your fingers stretch
from coast to coast to try it out,

this solitude, while water thumps
through the riverbed.

*

You're not exactly on your own.
Teenagers come and go, the screen-door

clacks, cardinals mob a little temple
hanging in a tree. A neighbour with a bag

of seeds asks you if you mind
the birds. There is that film, and the flu,

but no. In the mornings earlyish
you slide the rippling trees across

(Burnham Wood) and watch
six parrots lift like anti-gravity.

*

At sunset a rant about the dishes –
you've worked all day, unlike

some people! The tap runs. The sun,
tumbling over Waikiki, shoots through

the trees, gilds the stream (unnecessary),
stuns you in the empty room. Every day

or ten years (you realise, standing there)
you've crossed the bridge etched Mānoa

Stream, 1972, back and forth,
except the day the river rose.

*

Some facts: mongooses (sic) (introduced)
pee into the current, plus rats and mice,

the stream is sick. All the streams.
Mosquitoes – your messengers and those

that bit the teenagers whose young blood
is festive like the Honolulu marathon –

could carry West Nile virus. Often fatal.
Probably don't, are probably winging it

like you, and you will go your whole life
and only die at the end of it.

*

The stream doesn't *look* sick. It takes
a pretty kink near your apartment.

The trees are lush and spreading
like a shade house you once walked in

in a gallery (mixed media). The water
masks its illness like a European noble

with the plague – a patina, and ringlets.
You're pissed about the health issues

of the stream, and healthcare, because
it has your blood, you have its H_2O.

*

You think it's peaceful by the stream?
Ducks rage, waking you at 2am,

or thereabouts. Mongooses hunt
the duck eggs, says your son. Ah, you say.

That night the quacks are noisy, but
you fret in peace. Sometimes homeless

people sleep down by the river bank.
Harmless. One time one guy had a knife.

They still talk about it and you see him
ghostly like an app against the trees.

*

All your things are near the stream,
beds, plates, lamps – you're camping

5

apart from walls and taps and electricity.
Your laptop angles like a spade,

and clods of English warm the room
(already warm). They warm your heart.

Overall you have much less, because
of course – divided up. But you're lucky

or would be if the stream was squeaky
clean, and talked to you.

*

The stream had caused a little trouble
in the past, i.e., the flood. Not its fault.

900,000 people pave a lot, they plumb
a lot. Then rain like weights. From a safe

distance (your old apt) you watched
your little watercourse inflate and thunder

down the valley taking cars, chairs, trees.
You saw a mother and her baby rescued

from a van – a swimming coach, with ropes –
the van then bumbled out to sea.

*

One apartment in your complex
took in water in the flood. And mud. It was

this apartment. You've known it all along,
of course, because you watched.

They fixed it up. Lifted carpets, blasted
fans for a week. Repainted.

It's pretty good. The odd door
needs a shoulder still. In certain lights

though, on the wall, a watermark,
the stream's dappled monogram.

*

You're talking clichés – water under
the bridge, love letter from a lawyer,

serious harm, sunk without you.
The stream has been into your bedroom,

and you in its. Remember reeds, coolness,
summer afternoons. You loved

the stream. Its stinging waters send
a last message in lemon juice:

fevered me, infected,
flooded me.

If I'm fucked,
you're coming with me.

Sincerely,
the stream.

The Black Drop: My History of Ugly

Suddenly they're churning away from the misty sounds

in the little barque, drying books jawed-up with specimens

such as the tough leaf of a cabbage tree Joseph Banks

and Dr Solander classified according to Linnaeus's

look book and named *Cordyline banksii* because Banks –

who lost his trousers one hot night in Tahiti – is paying.

In the clammy cabin – think clotheslines of blotters –

he frets about the needling New Zealand rain:

damp will humus the specs as if they'd never left

their forest, and then what will be the point? Above all

the prizes must arrive home dry. (In Tahiti, by contrast,

the books were onion-skin under the Transit's moon.)

Days later on the boxy coast of terra nullius, Banks croaks

a private plea to father Linné (Jesus of the leaf, mentor

to Dr Solander), *Guide me!* And the barometer rises

like Eastertime. Meanwhile (no one knows this)

George III's Yankee penal colony will soon be dead,

long live the penal colony. And Banks steps ashore

at Botany Bay.

He dries the drying books open and open

under the fierce sun. By nightfall, saved, but more

cursedness: the *Endeavour* is broken, in dry dock! Also

the two remaining artists (one died in Tahiti) are poorly.

For seven weeks while the cartographer perfects his lines

and Cook his book of swells, all hazy with experiment,

Banks and Solander, solid with their ballast of Latin,

light on the red turf, their green and pleasant Bible

held up against the continent, and they find, classify,

name, take, for science's sake and for London –

where the repurposed coal hulks anchored offshore fester

with felons, the streets glister with whisky and piss.

The jewel of their findings – well there's the eucalypt –

a fat cock ridged in bumps, nothing girly, but serviceable,

dusky red, ochre yellow, can't miss it, obvious to bees,

and they call it *Banksia* because Banks (this is the chorus)

is bankrolling everyone – Dr Solander, the sickly artists,

five servants, their food, the materials – to the tune of £10,000.

Eventually they are churning back to England, all aboard

apart from the dead, all a success apart from that moment

in Tahiti when the Transit was simply a black drop and Banks looked past the physical world into nothingness.

Back home he stocks Kew Gardens with the shoots

of pure science, his star rises in the Royal Society,

his sphere of influence expands to *I see dead people*

and the colony is born.

Next – this is much later – I, at 21, hogget-reared product

of the grand design, travel back (nod my head at where ugly

comes from), step off the Tube at Kew to a rush of machine oil,

flowers, Mrs Dalloway, enter the vast botanical organisation

and on a winding path smell childhood colds and come upon

eucalypts peeling to a smooth sore pink like the skin

of an Englishman at the cricket downunder

and over there, *Banksia*, and across a small sea of bluegrass

a ludicrous leggy second cousin from home waving:

cabbage tree in an unaccustomed grove.

Two Waters

All winter the rain blubs on the shoulder of Ihumātao.
The main drag splutters under people's gumboots.

Children squeal and catch raindrops on their tongues
in the place where the cat got the tongue of their ancestors.

Everything is going on. Laugh and cry and yin and yang,
kapu tī and singing in the white plastic whare.

On the perimeter people hold hands in a tukutuku pattern.

The plans of the developers hologram over the lush grass.

Day and night, police cars cluster like Union Jacks –
red white and blue, and oblique, and birds fly up.

A hīkoi carries the wairua across the grey city.
Auckland Council can take a hike. It's the wettest winter.

The signatures of the petition sprout from the two waters.

The sky falls into the earth, the earth opens its memory.

An Hour

The person of the hour remembers a model of an atom
The person of the hour learned Japanese at school
The person of the hour used to grow peppers
The person of the hour sees that it is 8 o'clock
The person of the hour just earned the minimum wage less tax.
The person of the hour notices leaves turning at odd angles
The person of the hour's hands are veined with carbon
The person of the hour read an article about bees
The person of the hour sees that it is 9 o'clock
The person of the hour just earned the minimum wage less tax.
The person of the hour thinks about herd immunity
The person of the hour knows hospital corners
The person of the hour has a yellow jacket
The person of the hour sees that it is 10 o'clock
The person of the hour just earned the minimum wage less tax.
The person of the hour likes wool and weaving
The person of the hour cleans the staff bathrooms
The person of the hour has a mother who doesn't remember them
The person of the hour sees that it is 11 o'clock
The person of the hour just earned the minimum wage less tax.
The person of the hour bear-hugs their son at bedtime
The person of the hour's ironed sheet is a blank page
The person of the hour has blistered heels
The person of the hour sees that it is noon
The person of the hour just earned the minimum wage less tax.
The person of the hour thinks the new motorway is a disaster
The person of the hour plays cat and mouse with the sun
The person of the hour makes dresses at Xmas
The person of the hour sees that it is 1 o'clock

The person of the hour just earned the minimum wage less tax.

The person of the hour is not entirely happy with the local school

The person of the hour has a few last plastic bags

The person of the hour puts their back out falling

The person of the hour sees that it is 2 o'clock

The person of the hour just earned the minimum wage less tax.

The person of the hour diagnoses smells on the bus

The person of the hour makes a hundred sandwiches

The person of the hour is a third of the way through their degree

The person of the hour sees that it is 3 o'clock

The person of the hour just earned the minimum wage less tax.

The person of the hour loves the smell of a child's head

The person of the hour puts the alarm clock on the other side of the room

The person of the hour mops up other people's vomit

The person of the hour sees that it is 4 o'clock

The person of the hour just earned the minimum wage less tax.

The person of the hour reads novels about love and no-love

The person of the hour likes the feel of the road while driving

The person of the hour is acquainted with the bleats of a child's asthma

The person of the hour sees that it is 5 o'clock

The person of the hour just earned the minimum wage less tax.

The person of the hour likes the comedy festival

The person of the hour was rostered to work New Year's Day

The person of the hour voted for a ticket in the council elections

The person of the hour sees that it is 6 o'clock

The person of the hour just earned the minimum wage less tax.

The person of the hour likes baking bread

The person of the hour feels nervous in the building after dark

The person of the hour is worried about kids' uniforms

The person of the hour sees that it is 7 o'clock

The person of the hour just earned the minimum wage less tax.

The person of the hour star-gazes while emptying the bins

The person of the hour is going to a wedding in March
The person of the hour is being evicted from their house
The person of the hour sees that it is 8 o'clock
The person of the hour just earned the minimum wage less tax.
The person of the hour hopes their kid is in bed
The person of the hour remembers a hit song from 2006
The person of the hour drives to their other job
The person of the hour unlocks for the night shift
The person of the hour just earned the minimum wage less tax.
The person of the hour just earned the minimum wage less tax.

Fox and Hounds

1

In the summer you might end up going for a lager
at a pretty beer garden named for the slaughter

of the endangered red fox by marauding dogs
followed by boomy packs of rich folk on horseback

who own the dogs, the horses, the land where the fox
lived its short life. You might be interested to know

that in the UK it is no longer legal to let the dogs
tear the fox to shreds. It must be killed humanely

whereby the hunters dismount, walk towards the fox
in their high brown boots and shoot it in the head.

Meanwhile hunt saboteurs lay citronella to put the dogs
off the scent, and wires to trip the horses (poor horses).

You may end up wanting to tripwire the property
market because you hate the property market.

2.

You end up at an auction where young people bid
astronomical amounts for dumps in outer suburbs

which they could make into a home with a bit of work.
But the investor in the corner walks over in their boots

and bids and bids until they own all the houses. They
can't live in all the houses, they don't need all the houses

but they want them, and they can have them because
the policy-makers say that they can. They say, one day

we'll build more houses, we'll limit investing, and also
young people like flatting, they like houses the size of

a cupboard. Not us, but then, we've always had a house
we've always had a house with two bathrooms, a garden

and a garage in a nice street. Oh, and we have another
house, in the country, and the fox is half-dead.

These Scholars at the Picnic One Day

My poem about the hot day Susan and I

lunched by the river might be boring with just

us in it so I'll add a man, a scholar I think

and give him an elbow to lean on while talking

to my other invention, the other scholar

who'll be nutting out an ontological problem

and so gazing upwards glassily and of course

nestled up to me. But here's the thing,

just for a laugh I'll dress these scholars.

Yes, I'll give them black serge jackets

although it's like 30 degrees, grey flannel

trousers, thick shirts and cravats. Hey,

and a fez each, not to be pretentious

but they'll look a little pretentious

and perhaps even be a little and Susan

will go to swim half-dressed in the river.

I'll be a bit pissed at her for ditching me

and truth be told self-conscious at being left

the only normal one on the grass. In the

struggle to dress the men we've spilled

the picnic in the leaves so there's no food.

Eventually I'll realise that the first scholar

is not talking to the other scholar but to me

expounding on the nature of art. I will find

it boring and will be sorry I ever thought

to add these men to the lunch on the grass.

I will look away, I'll look, reader, at you

hoping you'll interpret my pleading expression,

take off your clothes and drop them one by one

on the grass as you come over

to rescue me.

Light On in the Garden

Dread

The guys on the exec team hate art.
They watch a movie sometimes, hum along to a tune in the car,
buy jewellery for their wives,
but the guys on the polytech executive team really hate art.
Sure they visit the Met when
in New York, used to moondance in their twenties,
and they all wear clothes,
but sadly the members of the polytechnic executive committee
hate art.

The problem is – and it's a very big problem – there is an art school
at the fucking polytech.
The art school is in an old chip factory, it is loud, fun and shocking,
and history and memory,
tragedy and beauty, argument and experiment, grief and comedy,
and the new
stream out in form and colour, sound and movement, writing and speaking
firstly into the garden
the garden of tyre sculptures sprouting with thought and work
and performance,
then into the local community, the parents, grandparents, aunties, uncles,
who already love art
who live art, in their houses, churches, halls, walls, streets, shopping centres,
then beyond into the city,
and the students at the art school think and wrangle and shape and say,
and the graduates

go into the world making and teaching and wrestling and theorising
about art.
The seven members of the polytechnic executive committee
with their various
chief executive academic provost professor business-partner headdresses
hear about the goings-on
at the art school – the entertainment, reflection, representation – and they are
filled with dread.
They are careful never to stray near the old chip factory
especially after dark.

The very reverend executive team all live as far from the polytechnic
as it is possible to live
while still being technically domiciled in the supercity because unfortunately
the polytech is situated
in a part of town that is quite problematic for a modern major executive.
It might look hip,
with its markets, food, music, dance, its elders sitting talking
in the shopping centre
at lunch time, but they are working people, they are brown and scary,
plus there are a lot of them.
The executive officials are therefore forced to live far away from
the community they serve,
from the people who pay with their hard-earned, three-job, clean-up-your-shit
taxes
the executive-sized salaries that spill down the shirtfronts of the pro-vices.
You might wonder
how the guys on the exec team manage to score a job where they earn
gigabytes of dollars
making decisions about a community they live a conurbationsworth
of ks away from

geographically, culturally, squeamishly – especially decisions
about art –
when they hate art? Well yeah. Every afternoon the directorial heads
squeeze their headdresses
into their sleek blue hybrids, merge onto the motorway
and drive home to their wives.
On Fridays they have their secretary send an email to the people
just letting them know
in a super-friendly way that they've had a good week educationing
with the minister
and that in the weekend they'll be tinkering in the garden shed,
entertaining the grandkids
watching the rugby and shouting Go the Blues at the blue TV.
We're blue
like a song. Yes, we've got the blues. Want to hear about our lives?
Will you listen
to where the notes fall on the petrol station forecourt after rain?
I have heard
the grass singing in the ebullient minds of the controlling officers.
I imagine
they are partial to the setting sun as they drive across the bridge
('look through your sunset hair
into my world / before I die / and collect your imaginary mind'),
the geometric pattern
of the carpark like a dance, the tukutuku panels in the marae,
they have seen
the undersides of leaves in their garden and looked up at the sky
through the trees
and that on some level the woolly superintendents of the polytechnic
love art.

Lies

Because there is art
let's imagine an esteemed attaché of the polytechnic
is harbouring something
in the privacy of his home across the harbour. What's coloured
and painty?
The painting charges into his life like a horse, a little scary
and exciting like sex.
It's hard to say what it is or isn't – a bunch of nerves. All he knows is
he likes it.
Which poses an existential problem for a man at a round table.
When people
come to the door, neighbours, someone collecting for the poor, it's,
Quick, hide the painting!
Dinner guests who've toured the house and garden enquire of the wife,
What's in there?
The high priest answers, Our hydroponics, where we hide the bodies
ha ha ha.
The kids are eyeballed across the table. Don't fucking mention
the painting
if you value your freedom. He loves this painting
but unfortunately
the fat controlling managerial officer
hates truth.

Imagine a member is driving home over the bridge
before dark
(in case he turns into a brown person)
sun in his eyes,
twiddling the radio dial back and forth and comes upon
music.

It rushes into his organs – his lungs, heart, brain, spleen –
and he is transported
in a different way from transport. He drives on, listening to the divine
noise
careful not to exceed the speed limit because if he got pulled over –
good thing he's white
so low chance but still, if he was breathalysed, it could be in the news.
On Tuesday evening
a field-marshal of the polytechnic was driving over the bridge under
the influence.
He keeps listening and driving carefully into the sun
and he loves this music
but the member of the polytech boss team remembers his official position
on beauty.

Imagine that one day while tinkering in the garden shed
dear leader
feels a new energy enter his body. He wants to move, sideways, up and down,
with a certain rhythm.
He tries to shut it down but it won't go away so he shuts the shed door
and in the light
from the window he begins to explore his range of movement
in space.

Among the tools and the lawnmower he uses more space
in more ways
than he ever knew was possible and as he moves his limbs he thinks about
history and memory,
tragedy and beauty, grief and love, and he finds that his body is somehow
dancing those things.
When he goes inside for dinner his wife says, You seem different,
and he says,

I'm the same, I am always the same and I will always be the same.
That night in bed
his feet cross and splay, pyjamas pirouette, his beautiful throat.
Dear, says his wife.
He clamps down the little motor of dance which has been running
inside him
since the afternoon and which he loves, he did love,
he loved the passion,
but that's all very well and the guy from the polytech exec team
hates truth.

Imagine they find themself –
one of the guys from the exec team – in the garden at night-time
looking up through the trees
at the sky noticing how the leaves are trembling in the moonlight
and they notice
the wind on their face, the earth beneath their feet and the scent of grass
and they begin to think
about being in this place. Their family is in the house – how lucky they are –
but how strange
that they are out here in the garden on their own feeling and thinking
in this moment
in time. And they think about nature, and then they think about
the nature of nature
and how humans might experience that, and by humans they mean
themself
and by themself they mean humans. And then they notice the outside light
how it throws light
and shadow on the garden and how that makes quite a big difference
to the garden
and they experience a little thrill at the idea that human intervention –
the invention of the light

and the fact the light is installed in the garden – so, ingenuity and practice –
changes
how we see the garden. And not just that, the history of all these things,
these feelings and thoughts,
didn't just pop out of nowhere, they are mixed up with their own history,
their childhood, family, work,
and how that bundle coming together creates this particular view
of the light in the garden
and how in turn this makes this human think and feel a certain way,
and words come,
they just do, in an apparent attempt to express this, to capture it,
to capture something –
the outside light, the fullness, the nothing, let's not, but we are half way there
or something.
They will work on it, it will be waiting for them to return to even when
they are not in the garden
and it is not night-time, and there is no light, it will still be there.
And they realise
they have been trying to put together actual art with the nature of art
in a garden
which is nature, and that is hilarious and exciting and they realise
they are in ecstasy
and they are filled with dread.

Art

Things have got to a very bad stage. They are hoarding beauty. They are hoarding truth.

They have been turning up at the polytechnic on Monday mornings ashamed, so ashamed, and not telling anyone at the coffee machine, or the admin person who brings coffee to the high-up teetering people. They straighten their ties (the odd woman who ended up in the wrong toilet does an equivalent clothing adjustment). They make sure no ecstasy appears on their face.

By the time he has the courage to admit it to himself, one enormous boss man has truth and beauty bulging out the door of his house and filling up the windows. Inside, it's hard to steer a path between the stacks of truth and beauty. Truth and beauty could fall on him and kill him. Rodents and insects have made nests in truth and beauty. The boss's wife and kids moved in with her mother long ago. He goes on a TV programme about people like him. He says on camera, I just can't let go of all this art, please help me.

On reflection, the members of the executive committee realise that the people in the old chip factory are to blame. Of course, the art school. This was always the case. The art school has been there for thirty years, and it is terrible. They are terrible people. Loud, monstrous. They make stuff up. They do pictures. They have flowers coming out of tyres.

Luckily there is a special playbook for shutting down art schools. The members of the executive committee get their PAs to look it up on the dark web. It goes thus: 1) Stop the art school from advertising so no one knows it exists. 2) Establish an enrolments target that rises steeply. Hell will freeze over before it can be achieved. 3) Make the lecturers responsible for a new business case even though there are employees called 'business partners'. 4) Ensure the lecturers work 60-hour weeks so they have no fight left. 5) Make the lecturers feel like pieces of shit. 6) Gradually remove all the facilities necessary for an art school, like performance spaces, running water for cleaning paintbrushes, offices, meeting rooms. 7) Scatter the students throughout the campus so they don't get to know each other. They will be lonely. This is called destroying the community.

Discuss the takeaway from this. Takeaway takeaway takeaway.

Hey, that could be a song.

Nooooooooo!

Angle into your car and scream back over the harbour bridge before sunset

leaving the people
with the night.

2

Shit-faced: The Epistemology of the Mask

I'm going down the road in my mask.
Feeling so good in my custom mask.
I pass various people in their masks.
Their various paper and material masks.

I'm drinking red wine through my face.
What was the question sorry, ask my face.
I'm sorry but your face is lack of face.
Oh my face is lack of lack? Read my face.

Well of *course* no mask signifies lack.
It's the mask people wear when they lack.
They traverse the badlands with their lack.
Seeing shadows on the wall, i.e., lack.

I'm going down the road in my mask.
Feeling so bad in my custom mask.
I'm Thelma or Louise in my mask.
I'll meet you in paradise in my mask.

Dog and Plague

Outside Light

Dusk and the kitchen shadows
hug their ceiling.

The dog waits
for the littlest clink.

It's rubbish night, a night
to remember –
makes me happy,
makes me sad.

The outside light
is covered in lace. A late moth
kisses the moony face.

The dog runs along the side path.
The trees are running
from the light.

Before the Election

Cross the street because she hates
other dogs. It's the breed!
Remembering stuff.
It's the quiet.

Dog obedience, class of 2013.
A woman told our dog off
for barking, week after week.
Hated obedience.

The leader of the opposition could be
prime minister. Faark! Owooowoooowooo.

Oh and our dog did well in her exam
but just got B. Fair enough – barking.

The woman's dog peed on the floor.
Got D. Huh huh huh huh.

Wonderful World

The dog across the road goes apeshit
and my dog's by the front door
ready to blow. That thing's gonna blow.

And I say to my dog, That's right,
you be the bigger dog. She slinks back
into the shady house.

What a good good puppy. She's
forty-five or thereabouts. I try

to be the bigger dog although I'm small.
Someone says, that dress suits you
it covers your scrawniness. I say to myself

one day I'm gonna let whatever's
down there in terms of noise
come right out.

Full Moon

The dog looks
at the mad cat.

No cat
no.

The vase is
its shadow

the black painting
a mirror.

There there
dog. The stories

you've heard.
That a cat

wants to
drink your blood.

The Vet

Cough cough cough cough
Tough dog tough dog tough.

Bred on the border where they made
Braveheart. That's her people.

She's a wee tough dog. Rabbits
can fuck right off. The vet

says drugs and later a drop
of kennel cough. But turns out

after going down, like a quick brown fox,
ten rabbit holes on the internet

I'm anti-vax, they just want
their beach house overlooking the dunes.

I step over my little dog lying
on the kitchen floor.

Teddy Bear

The kids walking by
with their parents
on a nice day

count the bears
in the windows
of the houses

with the curtains
and the rooms.

Inside the house
is a room

is a curtain
a window

a day
is a dog.

Pestilence

The first lockdown was like

the *Wahine* when I stayed home
and drew faces on blown eggs

while branches crashed past
and my mother read the paper
and her book all day
sitting in a chair.

In the Honolulu flood we sheltered
with the Kobayashis

with our sons trapped
at the school dance.

Later the dads drove through
the receding waters to get them.

We were shit-scared and so happy.

My Dog

It's my dog playing
dog. My dog

practising
being a dog.

Dog dog dog
all day and all night.

Yellow dog
on a grey path.

Oh dog my dog
why have you?

The dog
my dog.

Oh doggie
my doggie.

Overseas

I've had amazing times
camping
on planes.

My pillow my blanket my
dinner
on a plane.

I have amazing memories
of planes.

Once the man next to me
proposed to me on the plane.

That time we moved
overseas
on a plane.

Winn Dixie and the sun
setting
on a plane.

I'm probably
never going overseas again.

October

Dog is sick.
Poor dog.

Poor poor dog.
Love That Dog.

(Love that book.)
Heart

murmurs like a brook
or creek

seeing it's us
a long way

away. My little dog
her murmur

at the bottom
of the planet.

The Dreamers

When you wake up
you are in a place. It's as if overnight you swam through your consciousness
and everything that was not
this place has become this place. You call it Iowa. We will call it Iowa.
It's summer
and the streets shimmer like the old grainy American films you saw
in your old life
and you could be in a cinema, or even in a film, but it is Iowa.
Everyone is new.
It's as if you died and all the people you knew before are gone
and you wonder
if that's how it will be when you die. Oh Iowa, the milling crowd.
A kind woman called Mary
gives you a set of plates and cutlery and these will be your plates and cutlery
for all eternity.
You have conversations about books and food, places and love.
Iowa the elevator.
Fall comes on, and yellow leaves flutter down like a hologram.
You walk about
with your new friends in a walking bus, and you walk alone
as in a dream.
In the supermarket you dream you are in a supermarket.
People talk about
the president, they say, we're sorry for our president, and sometimes
wipe tears
from their eyes. Iowa the corn fields, the soy beans. You hear about
the Dreamers,
800,000 people who came to the US as children with their parents
for the American Dream,

who are undocumented, and the president wants to send them back
to where they were born.
At a rally at the Capitol, you hear Dreamers talk about their fear
of being sent back
to a place they've never lived, where they have no language
or knowledge or friends,
and that would be like dying or being in a film or dreaming
because America
is not their dream, it is their reality, and this is America.
One day squirrels appear.
They wag their fluffy tails and chase each other like creatures
in an American cartoon,
and you laugh. Iowa the comedy. The leaves have fallen and the wind
picks up and the people
you've met seem like the people you always knew. Iowa the dance floor.
The moment you realise
that Iowa is real is the moment you know you must go home.
And that is Iowa.

The Colour of the Grass: Notes on and off Decoration

In Santa Croce, 2007
'Your glory wears the colour of the grass' – Purgatorio XI ponders
how the artist is like a conduit which passes.

With this map I stood in front of the death of Saint Francis.

I was upright, he was prone, dead or at least dying.

We formed a cross, St F and I in the Cappella Bardi.

Everything I owned you could put your finger on.

The saint was attended by a keyboard of monks

and the great hand of Giotto.

Over the flag-stoned floor-saints went the new footsteps

of a girl who back home attended the academy of St Francis.

On pet day she took a rabbit to school.

To avoid the dead we (daughter and I) walked a Bargello pattern.

The chapter heading *Chapter Two. In Santa Croce with No Baedeker*

I had with me in my head in Santa Croce with no Baedeker,

and all of Forster and literature in English in general

jostling behind me like souls, like a soup kitchen.

I looked at the saint lying dying and felt sorry for him

for all the saints plying their various trades

in lost objects, hopeless cases, travellers, and in the case

of St F, the rabbit we might otherwise have eaten

if not for daughter's *over my dead body*.

A week before Christmas c1967 Mrs Basile no Old Mrs Basile

rocked towards me during Mass and kissed a deckle-edged

holy picture of the infant Jesus with dried flowers

still life from Italy and gave it to me.

I took it. By Christmas Day she was dead.

This was all the way across the world in the church of St Francis,

Island Bay, Wellington, New Zealand.

Summer in the half-light of the Basilica and I was peeling lightly.

A plaque said St F *et al.* had been plastered over for 200 years.

The communion of saints were considered too pretty by half.

Conservators chipped the saints free, and the angels, but some

of Saint F's Life came away leaving what was there before decoration

and no decoration.

In Santa Croce, Galileo and other hard men stuck fast in their bodies

like the statues of Narnia. The poet is not in his tomb.

Two men on a high scaffold ding at the altar

where light rushes in.

Someone gave us a pop-out map of Florence, its streets and monuments.

Also the Chair of Department (Italian) gave us a map and Cindy

a phrasebook and someone a long time ago gave Dante as if to say

Here's Heaven and Hell, etc., should you need them.

It sat for a long time as things put by in a freezer.

Someone said Hell has frozen over and I laughed

but it had not, it was still (*The Wild Things*)

hot.

In the beginning black mantillas formed a bloc beside white panama hats

in the concrete church, the crack of new pews settling rang out into the silence

like a sign. There was singing, and a long time, years, to suck on

modernist stained glass, the jellybean toes of Jesus, his cartoon cross,

anime stare.

In the odd corner retro statues from the old dark church

(which they sold to the Serbian Orthodox who turned it golden)

wore fine hands and expressions of empathy (this jolly life!).

A stack of holy pictures by the masters was shuffled and dealt out

like patience on a blond pew, bartered at Communion time

by a circle of under-sevens. The trump card

Jesus with real flowers and a deckle-edge *From Italy*

while the air droned with a sort of poetry.

I never swapped it.

Once a year they blessed the Italian fishing fleet.

The billowing priest speaking the runny language,

and the taste of salt as the boats clustered. Later in the church hall,

ladies a Pākehā plate. Finally (the end, fini, finito, finished),

this Life (of the saint), the steady hand (of the artist), the *grass* (of the poet)

the plastering (of the master plasterer), the translation (again, from the poet):

please take it all away! I can't stand that it will ever

be over.

The Arrivals

When we arrive at the lounge of everything

with our bags

handfuls of earth   the lives of our grandparents

in our memory devices

we expect an exchange of sorts   that is what

we expect

and I think everyone deep down expects

that we will not turn back

Through a high window we will connect stars

like line drawings

translate the sparkles of the poet

we will

sign the fascinating mouth of the speaker

we will sing

lyrics that someone thought were pretty good

we will sing them

and we will not turn back   we will not

When our footsteps awaken fresh

from a long

complicated journey during which the planet

slid otherwise

we will likely remember a dream we had once

and tell

a version of it to the next person and the next

and realise hopefully

they also have a dream to tell and we will not

do that thing

where we won't listen to anyone else's dream

we will listen

and interpret   signing   singing   saying

we will use

the wisdom disseminated by our devices

we will not turn back

we will not

if on arrival there is wringing of hands

we will shake hands

and in the eye of a storm we will make tea

with our brilliant

fading bodies we will do a variety of things

while we can

we will bed down on the steps of the assembly

if we have to

we will bed down in a court of law

and all beds

anyway are temporary and when we see

that

and realise we have travelled through the night

we have travelled

and are not turning back   that

will be the point

at which we will arrive

The Sea Walks into a Wall

Action

Island Bay has a new sea wall.
Old sea wall, new sea wall.

The sea used to love the wall.
Now it hates the wall, it hates
on it.

The sea crashes its glass onto the bar.
You watch from afar.

You'd take it all back if you could. Everything.
You'd go down there and you'd.

Island Bay has a new sea wall.
It's the wall to end all walls.

Everything

Everything is in small bits –
sand, salt, the air is glitter. The coast
took a long time to get pretty like this

but the people on the beach – you know them all,
family, friends, frenemies – are stopped in time.
The wall is one huge thing
sitting there.

On the sand: first it is warm then it gets cold.
I am a daughter of the wall. It's my
post-industrial wall and I stand by it.

Old sea wall, new sea wall.
You're watching from afar
the broken place where
your memories are.

All summer, children ran along the wall –
it's massive like a steam train from nineteenth-century Britain,
a replica of a wall in a seaside town

built 1938 (before the war)
the colony playing catch-up with the motherland,
a great grey road going nowhere.

The wall was: you're here, everything else is
overseas. It was a great wall.

The wall was your 70s platform shoes reaching down
through the lava, each step a biopsy: salt-fish, the warm sand,
Taputeranga, but sooner or later
hell.

The Tempest blows about on the wind. It's Island Bay
in reverse. At dusk the Neapolitan fishermen lean on the wall
smoking and looking out to sea.

Like a public bar
the old sea wall was so noir,
it was so
Marguerite Duras.

The children sing at Italian weddings in the new echoey plaster church.
Afterwards on the beach, shadows sprawl on the photos.
The brides try to tame their giant smoky veils
in the wind.

They bless the boats from the beach,
the beauty and the sinister billowing gown of the priest
who touched your hair in a small room.

Below the cliffs, the steampunk wall
waits for the sea. The sea can never break
me.

You love the wall.

You go down there and you.

Tāwhirimātea

The storms surprise like illness.

A short history of storms:

There was the storm that made us reminisce on summer evenings
about the storm. The night the night
screamed through the open window
and hid in the girl's room.

Curtains flung like a dance class at the barre.
The girl didn't know these girls.
The lightshade jerked insanely on its string.

She harbours them all night because who's to know? Everything
is new. At dawn the chimney flips its lid, aghast on the roof.

Rain makes a six-foot Rorschach on the rosy wall
chosen from a roll that a man in white laid out on a trestle
and with his white arm swung on the smell of glue.

The trip across the wet lino to meet the wind
head-on, full of wind (the window frame stripped back the wood
by the roar) the loneliest journey in a life
so far.

All day home and all day wild, the grey sky thick with things.
Your trees, your heart? They are, they aren't.
The windows growl like a worried dog.
On the beach, the long bodies lie.

The Italian fishermen
in the forte murk
back and forth
like Dunkirk.

Afternoon it's calm, but the ripped streets.
You go down there and you.
The wall stands but the road is beach. Never forget
safety broken like a soprano's glass.

Then there was the big storm, called the big storm
like the big lie.

Another Wall

A short history of walls:

In Vietnam the French colonials with the strip of land
where nothing grows – it's so harsh (the salt marsh).

Marguerite Duras: her mother does everything wrong.
She's a widow, stuck in Saigon.

With money she doesn't have, she builds a wall to stop
the deep seep of salt. But the wall

is secretly in love with the sea. Year after year
the salt water tickles the sea's feet.

The family is destitute. Marguerite's mother
goes mad. Plan B (post-wall) is dangle

Marguerite (aged 15) like bait in front of a rich man.
Local, of the land. He becomes *The Lover*.

At home in Island Bay, I read Duras, I read Jean Rhys,
Doris Lessing, all the fucked-up settler girls.

Sheltered, where the sea pounds its wounds
I love my wall and I'm beginning

to hate it.

Council v. Sea Wall

They call the 2013 storm the big storm even though no one died.
The sea wall crumbled like a cake.

You go down there and you

learn the time before the wall
when the soft dunes went with the sway
of the sea, there was nothing in way
of the sea. It nested up, rushed up, rugby-ed up
the bay.

There was a little fight.
They line up on either side.
The people who leaned on the sea wall want a sea wall.
The Council wants no sea wall at all.
They rebuild the wall.
The iwi bides its time.

The sea wants
itself
its own
sea shelf.

Probably.

The big fight is: the wall
will take you with it in the night.
In the end, just the sea,
the sand, no fight.

Act VI

You go down there and you.
Old sea wall, new sea wall.

Old sea wall was a statue of a wall.
It was warm and gritty.
The air is rough and blue.

Old sea wall was so blood and guts.
It was tender, it was stone.
It trembled with salt and light.

The wall was the gateway to the sea.
The wall was so grey.
All night and all day
it kept storms
at bay.

On the beach, always an aftermath of a wedding,
froth and a mess of ribbon and glass,
a runway for lost souls returning
a regret.

Tangaroa is like butter in the sun today.

I love the wall. I pummel the wall. My hands are on
the warm, grey, post-industrial wall.

In the next storm, the sea will take the wall
back into its real-time, moving, shining
thing.

My heart is like a wall
struck down in a storm.
You didn't even need that wall
at all.

3

What Fell

For Temuera

It was Fall in the Tropics or what
they call Fall. Nothing fell.
Every leaf a last leaf
painted onto a wall.
Memories settled gently
onto the array of islands.
Learning American-as-a-second-
language the boy asked, What falls?
Well, mist falls onto the hills
of Honolulu. Rain falls.
Fumes fall on downtown.
The pens of the students
at the elementary
land on the page each morning,
their hands fall onto their hearts
in allegiance to the flag.
The school day flutters slowly
downwards to hometime.
Planes fly in from LA bringing
everything. The sun sinks
quickly below the horizon
leaving a green lip like
a mussel.
The Hep B shot fell
into the boy's arm. Ouch!
The rising inflection of sentences
was inverted to become
a falling.

Once people from the continent
of America fell, fell, down into
the Pacific bringing their prized
sicknesses – ouch! – and their homesickness
for Fall and in their agony
they called nothing falling Fall
even though the leaves fell gradually
throughout the year
without fuss or comment.
Of course, there was The Fall
which is perhaps what they
really couldn't live without.
And going right back, that time
the sun exploded and the fallout
created the solar system
its stars and planets
and the animals on the land
and the fish in the sea
and the thoughts in our heads
and the living and the dead
rising and falling.

The Book of Changes

For Sally Rodwell and Alan Brunton

The superior man house-sits on a hill

At your friends' house you're cast as a man
again and again in the big dark rooms.

Masks, puppets leer from the walls.
Rows of costumes are Robin Hood green

and there's a foxed copy of the *I Ching*.
You swagger over and throw three coins.

The sun drops suddenly at seven o'clock.
The house steps over into night.

It becomes habit, wear and tear and the
loudness of the applause. Our stuff

is bubble-wrapped, we have no shelter,
and I am a man. Thank you.

The superior man returns to a childhood haunt

Coming to the place formerly known as home
and knowing every inch of the playground
intimately. Smelling again the scorched sand

against the sea wall. No sand as definitive,
no dirt so boy. Forty years close over.
Was it better when the wound was fresh?

Uninterrupted view of the superior man

From the house I saw six figures in the sky.
It was the outlook for the next day. Surprise!

Some people have a tender, spongy vision
you think you could squeeze but you can't.

Then it all gets played or said or written down
– i.e., it's gone. All the plans become plans.

Once I heard birdsong that'd been recorded
and played backwards over and over.

Now there's something concrete.

Notice I say 'is'. It outlasted the bird.

The superior man remembers something random

Once I saw a young woman pushing a baby
(I think it was a baby) in a big old-fashioned
pram cocooned in white and silver shawls

like a nursery spider's web, lovingly,
under the railway bridge on the roaring
Great North Road. The word 'indices'

came to mind from maths at school.

I guess that baby's grown up now.

Change brings prosperity to the superior man

The first change was the purpling of nipples
and feeling the wind cold on them, the second
knowing what the first change was. The third

change was feeling sick and the fourth growing
bigger, the fifth a new flat, and then I lost count

except to know that cells in young bodies
grow fast and we are withering slowly.

They changed schools, they change friends,
teachers, neighbours, street, cities. Aue!

We cling to the changes that we know.

The superior man agonises about her children

The last walk to the kids' school was walked
in the same way as the first walk, noticing
every leaf, crack, the rage of the motorway.

The last night in the house was slept as the
first was, everything foreign and undone.

The last trip to the supermarket was a little death.

What to do with all the times in between,
passed now, but not first or last?

The superior man gets everything wrong

I thought it was that aria ('Remember me')
but it was the washing machine on spin.

I thought it was a pipe band but it was
a siren heading down The Parade. I thought

it was the waves but it was a memory
of the north-western motorway.

I thought it was the bells ringing out
from St Joseph's, the Mrkusich church.

It was dial-up knocking on the door
to the internet. I thought it was a child's

sleeping breath curving out into the hall,
but it was the wind in the trees from the

earlier fairy tale. If you hear these things,
please, tell them where we are.

In the Way

Without distractions you'd rush through your life like chi through an
  empty room.

You bump into a baby and that takes up eighteen years.

Love fills the room like a maze.

Japanese screens fold into your life.

You'd be dead otherwise.

Marriage took up twenty years give or take.

Lies someone told you took two years.

You spend an afternoon in the Hamilton Gardens.

For several months you hold the car door open for toddlers.

Weeks watching the progress of mercury in a thermometer.

Several years the pages of critical theory kept you from death.

A poem kept you from death.

A big wind gathers out at sea.

There's another thing like a box and you don't know what's in it.

You walk together in the forest and the forest is a thing.

You sit on the sofa together and read books.

She's the passive character to whom things happen.

Christmas is a red and green thing to go around each year.

Without distractions you'd rush through your life like chi through an
empty room.

Love fills the room like a maze.

Small objects appear underfoot and you deal with them in turn —
you have to.

When there's a problem you act but your action has the opposite
effect to what you thought.

The wind rushes across the room.

The family are like dogs.

They are all over you like me me, I've been waiting all day to see
you, and so-so happy.

Sometimes you stand on them by accident and they squeal and snap
with their perfect white teeth.

That's how the parents are.

Love fills the room like a maze.

The children copy their parents until the middle period when they
try to be the opposite but when they get older they're too busy to
think about that anymore and they go back to being like dogs.

She is worried she will never get to the thing.

When they were young the whole thing was sex.

The mother held the car door open and was patient like a dog.

The father looked out the gate and snarled.

Sex was the alpha male.

Sometimes they went for a walk in a forest if they happened to be passing
  on a road trip.

The fragrance of trees slowed them down.

Without distractions you'd rush through your life like chi through an
  empty room.

The children came from sex so the whole thing is disgusting.

They're all like dogs left in a house to survive.

You hope they break free and someone looks after them.

Without distractions you'd be at the end of your life before you were ready.

Warp and Aho: A Part-life in Flax

For Eileen Te Aho

Harakeke / lily really

In the beginning   an app for flax   in the soil   is family   the proverb
    a cute shoot   raised by wolves   hey it's the Pacific   the loving state
o nanny my nanny   wonder no wonder   fibrous as hell   later   baby
    in the middle   oldies on the outside   getting ragged   dew runs down
the blue arms   midsummer   the yellow parties   down in the garden
    a wild section   when winter comes   winter   alone and moonlight
writes the harakeke   no one sees   or hears the cells   burst their height
    but in the morning   no doubt   the dead of night is   is a factory

When a girl   not her   but always   some   body   is colonised
    and coloniser   two in one   seriously   too much girl too   part
lateral thinker part straight line   pretty much   covers everything
    like a mat   I want to say   nothing   about a book   the library one day
about the long   roa   as in Aotearoa   and strong   steampunk strands
    reaching back   industrialised like crazy   and forwards   sometimes
dyed   almost blue   the river too   the eternal thread   is te aho
    whenu the length   aho the strength   before going   any further

I fucking   love   textiles   run between   the fingers   dial up
    a childhood of linen   abuse   and love   gusts   Irish ghosts
lace on acid   everyone cool with?   silence and beauty
    warp and weft   whenu and aho   on her other side   similar ravage
what I hope   what I think GLAM*   hopes   remember   things

---

* galleries libraries archives museums

keep the plastic   write about the plastic   on the plastic
the unbelievable touch   must never be broken   but will be broken
        the museum library   sheds   its particles   into the material world

Coloniser's chorus:

>*Ah begorrah,*
>*we like the flora*
>*we like the flora*
>*ah begorrah.*
>*We will send our*
>*genteel gunners*
>*to preserve our*
>*able runners*

Btw harakeke   is not a flax   is a variety of lily   *Phormium tenax*
    linen is a flax is a flax   related   through their rhyming side   surprise
DNA of the tongue   like most Pākehā   I love *the bone people*   *Bulibasha*
    hate   Public Works Act 1928   death rate   of the Māori Battalion
vote   left white left   but   but Te Aho   the confluence   pulls me
    eternal tug   who went   to the museum library   in a whakapapa way
the family way   spiralling after her   even though   I came   before
    I have tumbled   into the river   the garden   Kororāreka   the district court
in the library   a view of concrete   a new view of   her imagined enormity
    the flax   is my text   I will be quoting substantially   from the harakeke

Kaupapa / fantastic

Your history   fevered babies   with turncoat blankies   the ferny place
    you lay your head   gone from the light   land blackened   with ink

70

history is   the stuff you like   passed early   rain   in young graveyards
     the shaved fields   silt foreshore   your people buried   the slow sun
at the moony library   urupā   the good ghosts   are mischievous   I read
     in Te Rangihiroa   re harakeke   how they cut down the grandparents
unspeakable acts   muka / scrape   whītau / beat   soak dry   roll cord
     soak pound rub   rinse and repeat   Purgatorio for strands   at this point
there is no distinction   between whenu and aho   what they will become.
     Meanwhile linen   similar   the word mordant   is to dye   a horrible
colour   joking!   a time to dye   Purgatorio for Pākehā   in the library
     in my white gloves   blue balloons really   I break out   the ephemera
the light   fluttering   gooseberry seed   documents   Pākehā harvest
     their particular   loss   how-to books   order books   for rotted garments
the conundrum   holds everything in check   'Miss Mulvany has a very good
     eye for colour'   the death of colour   eternal life of colour   its death

    Ah begorrah
    we like the flora ...

Nau mai   did you know there's no   raranga ephemera   just weaving
     and books   sometimes I bust out   the revolving doors   of the library
example 1   Paula Morris   name-drop   in the garden   between showers
     tends the grandparents   laid out   on the concrete   the good long   roa
harakeke fronds   she washes the bodies   tenderly   next time I see them
     pūtī   dyed waiporoporo   in a vase   on a windowsill   On Display
backdrop Auckland city   clunk   like a mascot taken around the world
     photographed   at the top of the Eiffel Tower   and put on Facebook

'General remarks on mordanting.   It is absolutely necessary   before
     [the flowers of friendship faded   friendship faded (Gertrude Stein)]
any kind of yarn   yarn is mordanted   it should be thoroughly washed
     otherwise the results   will be disappointing.   Your yarn will not be
brilliant   [GLAM is so steampunk   historical-industrial-fantastical]

or if they are   it will only be for a time   and then   they will fade
and then they will fade' (Grasett).   GLAM is so honest   preserving
    ideas about things   GLAM preserves ideas about death   GLAM is so
hopeful   a pūtī is a pūtī is a   but what if   the outer leaves   leave
    when the shoots   are shoots   is there a   a whakataukī for that?

Ringaringa / tenterhook

Got threads   now is   nau mai   the forest   nau mai the mesh
    of earth and sky   now is the hour   for things   for things to get
material   to get   complicated   Tāniko   is the weaving method
    commonly used for borders.   'Once [in a blue moon]   the beginner
has become more familiar   with tāniko   one should create   new
    new   patterns   rather than copy   the old ones' (Mead).   Whatu
is a system of   of finger weaving   a cord stretched   between two
    two pegs   warp threads hung down   finer weft threads   between

Europeans seriously   pretty much   the same   except they call
    pegs   tenterhooks   ['she never throws away   any piece of paper
upon which she has written' (Gertrude Stein)]   'this is to certify that
    Sybil Mulvany has completed a training course   in spinning   dyeing
['the long light shakes across the lakes' (Tennyson)]   weaving plain
    weaving patterned weaving carpet tapestry' @London School of Weaving
takes a job at Taniko Weavers   3 Darby St   Auckland   tablecloths
    curtains   tea runners   doilies   lustre bridge cloths   Ruapekapeka

    Ah begorrah,
    we like the flora ...

Example 2   from life   Reina Whaitiri   clunk!   embroiders linen
    and fine cotton   the borders   tahi rua toru   pūtī   whā   manu

a tablecloth   by her own   hands   planted   in fine cross-stitch
    at a certain   time of year   I   hang it as a curtain   in the place
the place where the setting   sun   plummets   through the window
    blinding   us   temporarily   between seven and eight   at a certain
time of year   the time of year   Christmas   when the years gather
    like pin-tucks   and always   Reina's flowers   exes   in flax

In the language   mosh pit   where she jives   no other   party
    every   body   in fashion   from the chain stores   as the night
nears its heart   material flies   through the darkness   graceful arcs
    para   is   a tussock rain cape   always was   the big gold Rangipō
raincoat glittering on the Desert Road   behind cloud   the noon sun
    pours its quiet   accustomed breath   para is not the stretchy sound
of Para Rubber   Company   the long ring of cash   the waah of traders
    on the floor   not the sound   of the long   roa   white   noise

The strange zone   strange light   cast by the trellis   earth and sky
    fine threads create   create the backdrop   for a hui   a garden party
creepers   clamber   in the rogue atmosphere   ['the wild cataract leaps
    in glory' (Tennyson)]   where blood and mud   roses and berries   in
the fine weave   make a tāniko   tāniko pattern   remember   girl
    whenu the length   te aho the strength   warp the length   ['I returned
to a long strand' (Heaney)]   weft the strength   there is no   botanical
    relationship   between flax   and harakeke   and flax   and harakeke

Tāniko / kiss kiss

Her name   the eternal thread   from the lips of the father   on first sight
    of course she complains   ah names   you   that puppy   a playfight
on the grass   a part life   with sounds   people ask at airports   why two
    why   this white space   this white face   sometimes   they call her tea

73

always   always mystery   a story   of broken   severed   and taken
        and broken   always   questions   of the part life   in concrete
she is down there   in the garden   night and day   summer   winter
        and this is the hour   pō atarau   now is the hour   to get imaginary

It is morning   the white cloth   on the table   handed down   in sunlight
        through the red glass   Victorian door   the girl saw   once   in a dream
a burning woman   the house   ancestor of the gum fields   in Pākehā
        title   is insured   but not for   loss   on the long   roa   visa form
which she believes   she should not need   should cross   the border
        tāniko   as citizen   of the Pacific   is she   Ms or Miss   eternal
love   the land   cried at night   but she has   in the rain   a degree
        her law kete   her philosophy kete   her great knowledge   of loss

        Ah begorrah,
        we like the flora ...

In the museum of wild thoughts   kiss kiss kiss kiss kiss   puffs
        of ephemera   passing over the landscape
documents because   Ruapekapeka   documents because
documents because   Gate Pā   because

In the weaving   whenu and aho   warp and weft   the relationship
        the relationship between   harakeke and flax   is not botanical
is one of fineness

in the garden   the isolated tender shoot   exposed to the rain
        is the app   for the artwork   for the basket of knowledge
at this point there is no distinction between whenu and aho   what they will become

but for Miss tea   it has been   decided   the pour of sunlight
from the mouth of the father   she is   te aho

kiss kiss kiss kiss kiss kiss kiss kiss kiss kiss kiss

but now   e hine   ināianei   go out go out into
the pouring rain   the deafening white rain   sheltered   your   on
tenterhooks sheltered   by the sound   the sound   of your tīpuna

the being of te aho   expressed as an idea   something she isn't   a material thing
which will pass must pass   and will pass back again to the idea
and become the being of   te aho
the girl   will lose everything   but hopefully only at the end
and there will be no end   because te aho

Sea Wall Canticle

In memoriam, Claire Brookes, 1937–2003

1

Who will tell the history of her voice
now it is sung? I will. I will.

A soprano, a singer in ten million they said
when she won the same scholarship

Kiri Te Kanawa won years later. She said
no thanks in her ten-millionth tones

I'll stay home with my new husband
the Flying Dutchman not go to London.

Goodbye Gilda goodbye Tosca
goodbye Anna Elvira Susanna Contessa

her costume constructed of
the growing bones of children.

2

Sixty-four they bought a villa, old, and Franz
set about making it new across the road

from yours truly. In the streetful
of boys my mother said there're girls

moved in why don't you go over
I said I haven't been introduced yet

looked out the gate – a concrete mixer
cleared its throat, up close the last tendrils

of a borer bomb, ladder and nails,
scales and arpeggios, girls, a boy.

I went across, snuggled in next to Helen
and stayed for the rest of my childhood.

3

In Island Bay she was famous, the young
woman with the voice like Schwarzkopf.

My mother said Claire's voice sent
shivers down her spine, which was

a good thing. When she practised
the Flannerys, the Backhouses, the Zivkoviks

came out to stand in the middle of the road
disregarding the traffic. At Mass

people, strangers, craned up to the choir loft
looking for answers. Who was she?

She could've filled the Albert Hall
but she didn't.

4

One time she said imagine
if we were in Heaven

there'd be no illness and the chemist
would be out of a job

to nobody in particular or to
six or seven children as she

pegged nappies into the
singing wind. I said

if we were in Heaven we
wouldn't need to work.

She smiled and was
from that moment my mentor.

5

They called the last baby Elisabeth
with an 's'

after Elisabeth Schwarzkopf
her voice gone now

from the Staatsoper, from La Scala
from the Arena di Verona

from Glyndebourne, Covent Garden
from the Lincoln

Center
and from the middle of the road

but remembered
like Claire's.

6

I went with them everywhere.
Princess Bay every day

in the summer in the little bomb
looking through

the hole in the bottom
at the road rushing before

your eyes. Visited the cousins
as if I were a cousin.

Enough children to fill
a classroom playing

while the mothers gabbed
in their sisters' voices.

7

She ran choirs, all her life, choirs
St Mary of the Angels choir St Francis

de Sales choir adult choirs children's
choirs Christmas a busy season for choirs

like shearing (*Christmas comes in summer,*
hay is dry and tethered). She'd conduct

the grown-ups at midnight home by 2am
back at 8am for *Pa ra pa pum pum.*

She mixed the Christmas cake
at three in the morning

that was the only occasion
of silence.

8

For her girls she made shocking
pink coats lined with sponge which

stood up on their own to wear to Mass
on Christmas morning. (The coats

could've attended without girls.)
The sponge was sticky, hard to sew

so Claire sprinkled the seams with powder
to ease their path under the needle.

Where have they gone, the coats
the choir practices? What she taught:

you practise and your life is practice for
the pleasure of Christmas morning.

9

If she was a singer she was a talker. Talk!
about dancing with Franz

at the Dutch Club and from that moment
knowing

about her bachelor friend the scientist
who for lunch put a tomato between

two pieces of bread and squashed it
so Claire introduced him

to a girl she knew who became his wife
and they had many children and neat

sandwiches. About the lessons with
Dame Sister Mary Leo which bore fruit.

10

The other mothers lost
their teeth after the first

three or four kids but
for Claire an opera-loving

dentist pitched a tent
in her mouth and with

a light went
underground as if

this were Athens.
A singer needs

good architecture to resound
into the civilisation.

11

At our place was Jimi Hendrix
on the stereo at their place was

Remember me? Remember me?
on a radiogram

like a Dodge.
Never forget.

At our place was Is-this-chair-green-
or-do-we-just-think-it-is?

(It was green moquette with rolled arms
and was quite comfortable.)

At their house
was Claire.

12

Mornings she taught music
at the convent school and swung

her music case down The Parade
smiling at the top of her voice

singing an aria to the gods
the cheap seats

the pōhutukawa trees
to the applause of the sea

and the curved stalls of the sea wall
while her children cringed *Mum, don't sing!*

And me. I felt loved enough to be
embarrassed by her happiness.

13

Got the school choir to sing
The Silver Swan,

who living had no note,
when death approached

unlocked her silent throat.
Over and over.

A warning.

14

Taught Helen and me theory of music
like taking a clock to bits its

ticking strewn on the evening paper.
In a row on the couch us our

sticky staves pencils rubbers sheltering
from the noisy houses from Bob Dylan

Frank Zappa and the smell of finger paint
epilepsy and the mysteries of the rosary.

One night she took us to the Sonic Circus
at the university Poetry for Chainsaws

at Civic Centre. I would've been
into the poetry if it weren't for the music.

15

Sometimes I'd ring her up and say
What's this?

Ta de *da* da da da daaa,
Ta de *da* da da da *daaaa*.

It's 'Caro nome' from *Rigoletto*.
Daaa da da-a da, da da da-a-a *daa*-da-da?

'Ombra mai fù' from *Serse*. Of course.
We listened to the Brandenburg Concertos

on a Moog synthesiser (1975)
and preferred them

and thought
Bach would have too.

16

Among all the girls they had one son
Philip and they buried him young.

On the morning they got the news
my mother looked out the window

at their house and said there's something
wrong I know it, set about making scones.

Their Philip and our Philip
people shook their heads and said

both Philips gone. There was
some comfort in the fact we'd

all lost Philips, it was
almost normal.

17

At Easter the tone-deaf priest
could walk in tune

because Claire.
An everyman tenor

burst like a trumpet.
Anyone anyone

can sing said Claire.
The bass sang

My God, my God,
why have you

abandoned
me?

18

The last time I saw her she said
this is my sitting room I've never had

a sitting room before and I would
so like to have sat down!

And opened its doors like Paradise opening
onto her grand-daughters in the distance

coming home from St Catherine's
three twenty-five precisely she waved

like clockwork the daily silent
practice of loving for that

special event if ever
no even no eventually she said.

19

She once knocked over a tea trolley
at a gathering in the convent (pink parlour

I wasn't there). She told me about
the instant of contact the cold steel

the swell of sound the tremble
of crockery the moment

of knowing the teapots were going to go
the cups and saucers the milk and sandwiches

how that moment stretched out
into eternity.

Ever after there was a stain
on the pink carpet and whenever

she visited the pink parlour
for gatherings she would remember

the joyful mysteries the sorrowful mysteries
Anna Elvira Susanna Contessa

the Dutch Club Elisabeth with an 's'
everyman and the tone-deaf priest

the choirs the choirs the cakes the theory
and the Sonic Circus, the pōhutukawa trees

and the sea wall, this is what she remembered.
My God, my God and imagine

we were in Heaven. *Why have you?* The silent throat
unlocked. Remember, remember, now

it is sung.

Notes

'Flood Monologue': The 'shade house' refers to an installation by artist Maureen Lander in collaboration with poets Robert Sullivan and Briar Wood, exhibited at the Whangārei Art Museum in 2004 with accompanying exhibition catalogue.

The lines quoted in 'Light On in the Garden' ('look through your sunset hair / into my world / before I die / and collect your imaginary mind') are from an unpublished manuscript by my late brother, Philip Kennedy.

'The Dreamers' was written while I attended the 2017 Fall Residency of the International Writing Program at the University of Iowa (funded by Creative New Zealand). During my stay, the Trump administration threatened to remove rights granted by President Obama under DACA (Deferred Action for Childhood Arrivals), whereby 'Dreamers' – undocumented adults brought to the US as children – can remain in the US and apply for residency.

'The Colour of the Grass' refers to Dante's line, 'Your glory wears the colour of the grass' (*Purgatorio* XI.115–16).

Basilica di Santa Croce (The Basilica of the Holy Cross) is a principal Franciscan church in Florence where many historical figures, including Michelangelo, Machiavelli and Galileo (a late addition), are buried. There is a memorial tomb for Dante but his remains are not there, as he was exiled from his native Florence and is buried in Ravenna.

In E. M. Forster's novel *A Room with a View*, Chapter Two is called 'In Santa Croce with No Baedeker'. The young protagonist,

Lucy Honeychurch, abandons her guidebook as if casting aside the restraints of her education.

In 'The Sea Walks into a Wall', the reference to Marguerite Duras is about her novel *The Lover* which is based on Duras's real-life story of growing up near Saigon under French colonial rule.

In 'Warp and Aho', 'warp' refers to the longitudinal strands in weaving and 'aho' is the Māori word for weft, or the cross strands. This poem was the result of researching weaving techniques as part of an event for Tāmaki Paenga Hira Auckland War Memorial Museum and the Auckland Writers Festival in 2017.

These books were used as background to the poem:

Evans, Miriama & Ranui Ngarimu, *The Art of Maori Weaving: The Eternal Thread – Te Aho Mutunga Kore*. Wellington: Huia, 2005.

Grasett, K., 'Scouring and Dyeing with Vegetable Dye Recipes'. London School of Weaving, 1940? Auckland War Memorial Museum Library, MS-2003-54.

Grasett, K., 'Warp Making, Setting up a Loom, Weaving, Finishing or Waulking, and Pattern Drafting'. London School of Weaving, 1940? Auckland War Memorial Museum Library, MS-2003-54.

Hakiwai, Arapata & Huhana Smith (eds), *Toi Ora: Ancestral Māori Treasures*. Wellington: Te Papa Press, 2008.

Hiroa, Te Rangi (P. H. Buck), *The Evolution of Maori Clothing*. New Plymouth: Board of Maori Ethnological Research, 1926.

Mead, Sydney M. (Hirini), *Tāniko Weaving: Technique and Tradition – Te Whatu Tāniko*. Auckland: Reed, 1999.

Mulvany, Josephine & Sybil Mulvany, 'Order Book of the Taniko Weavers'. Papers, 1916–57, Auckland War Memorial Museum Library, MS-2003-54, Folder 1: Order book, 1929–32.

Other lines referenced in 'Warp and Aho' are from the following sources.

Stein: lines quoted are from the poem 'Before the Flowers of Friendship Faded Friendship Faded: Written on a Poem by Georges Hugnet' by Gertrude Stein, 1931.

Tennyson: lines quoted are from the poem 'The Splendour Falls' by Alfred, Lord Tennyson, 1848.

Heaney: line quoted is from the poem 'North', from the book of the same name by Seamus Heaney, 1975.

In 'Sea Wall Canticle', 'Poetry for Chainsaws' refers to a work by Jim Allen which was performed by the artist at Sonic Circus 2, a musical extravaganza organised by Jack Body that took place in Wellington, 8 March 1975.

Acknowledgements

Some of these poems, or versions of them, have appeared previously. My thanks for the following: 'Sea Wall Canticle' (under a different title) and 'What Fell' in *Poetry New Zealand*; 'Flood Monologue' and 'The Black Drop' in *Cordite*; 'The Arrivals' in *Poetry*; 'Two Waters' in *Poetry New Zealand Yearbook 2020*. 'An Hour' was written for an event as part of the Living Wage Movement Aotearoa New Zealand at the Newtown Festival, 2016.

Grateful thanks to the Estate of J. C. Sturm for permission to include the poem 'Untitled' from *Dedications*.

Thanks to Manukau Institute of Technology, where I was a lecturer in creative writing for eight years, for awarding me five weeks' research time, which was used to write some of these poems.

My deepest thanks to: everyone at AUP, especially publisher Sam Elworthy, editor Sophia Broom – for expert, thoughtful and kind care with the text – and Katharina Bauer; editor extraordinaire Elizabeth Caffin; proofreader Louise Belcher; designers Philip Kelly and Carolyn Lewis for their beautiful work. I am much obliged to the staff at Te Pātaka Mātāpuna Auckland Museum Research Library. To friends and family, especially Temuera and Eileen, arohanui always.

Anne Kennedy is the author of three novels, a novella, four books of poetry, and many anthologised short stories. Her first book of poetry *Sing-song* was named Poetry Book of the Year at the 2004 Montana New Zealand Book Awards. *The Darling North* won the 2013 New Zealand Post Book Award for Poetry, and *Moth Hour* was a poetry finalist at the 2020 Ockham New Zealand Book Awards. Anne has also won the BNZ Katherine Mansfield Short Story Award and has held fellowships at the University of Auckland, the IIML and the University of Hawai'i. She has taught creative writing for a number of years in Hawai'i and Auckland.